BEFORE OBLIVION

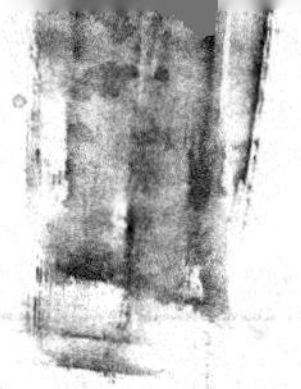

¡AN CANON

Ian Canon is an Edmonton novelist, poet, and essayist working in digital marketing with an obsession for storytelling in all forms. He is primarily interested in themes like existence, death, love, art, technology, and the mundane. His personal interests include politics, film (P.T. Anderson, Charlie Kaufman, Stanley Kubrick), poetry (Rudyard Kipling, Allen Ginsberg, E.E. Cummings), and fiction (John Williams, David Foster Wallace, George Orwell). He received a Bachelor of Arts from the University of Alberta in Philosophy and English.

JAI TANNINEN

Born and raised in Ontario, Jai Tanninen was interested in art and images from a young age. He spent most of his time drawing and consuming print images during childhood before beginning to paint in his adolescence. In 2008, after university, he traveled Canada until landing in Edmonton. Here, while observing the emergence of new frontiers in culture around him, he developed his own artistic practice. His work explores the complexities of human identity. He paints or draws from found imagery, exploring the possibility of implied narratives and emotional expression. He wants to explore the connections between image and meaning, and the formal aspects of colour and composition in image making. He imagines a world where, while the artist acts from their own experiences, the viewer can establish their own connections between themselves, the artist, and the world around them. Where they can reflect on the effects and value of experiences and the systems by which we represent them.

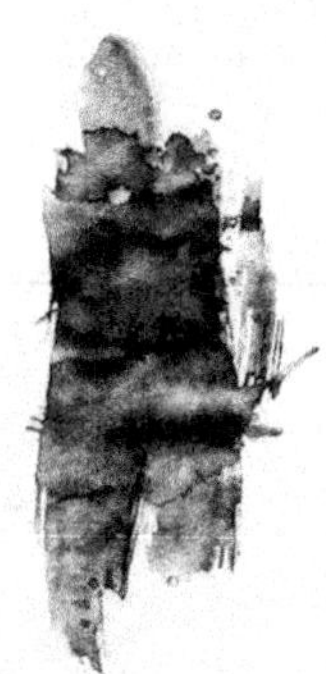

A BRIEF INTRODUCTION

BY IAN CANON

There is, I believe, a companionship that exists between the painter and the poet — an overlapping sensibility towards the world.

The poet Robert Creeley said, speaking of artist Francesco Clemente, with whom he frequently collaborated, "Any person reading what I've written and seeing what he's made is moving back and forth between two emotional fields. It's not a question of understanding, but of picking up their vibes."

In *Before Oblivion*, it was and is our goal to shift our dear viewer through a rhythmic dance of emotional states, discovering for themselves the simultaneously loose and close connections between the two mediums as both a single art piece and as their own individual movements.

But what are these movements and where did they originate? There were, in both our bodies of work, inherent thematic similarities that immediately stood out. As Wallace Stevens said, "The problems of poets are the problems of painters."

But to press the dialogue further, Jai looked over my entire body of work and picked out the themes that he felt would work best as a collaborative piece. At that point we separated and produced 16 poems and 16 paintings, then a year later, we added another 5 poems and 5 paintings.

Now we have a book with 21 poems and 21 paintings, from varying points in our lives, both made collaboratively and individually, and offering our own unique perspective on love, sex, art, masculinity, addiction, boredom, and the inevitability of death (oblivion).

Enjoy.

TABLE OF CONTENTS

2   ALL THIS SHRUBBERY

6   SHE SAID, SOFTENING

7   RAISON D'ÊTRE

10 THE HUMAN CONDITION
    IS ABSURD BUT CHARMING

12 THE LAST GOODBYE

14 CHIMERAS

16 MONSTERS, TITANS, GIANTS

18 A SINGLE MAN

20 A LIFETIME OF IDLENESS

22 BRICK WALLS

26 SUBLIMITY

28 IS ART

30 TWILIGHT

32 FALL APPROACHES

34 THE DAMNED HAVE SUCH BEAUTIFUL EYES

36 TOY SOLDIERS

38 EMPTY

40 ENTROPY

42 REAPER

44 PURGATORY

46 TO ALL YOUNG WRITERS

ADDICTION

THE INEVITABILITY OF   LOVE
DEATH (OBLIVION)

                           ART

SEX

BOREDOM

                    MASCULINITY

ALL THIS SHRUBBERY

and where once there was the tender-hearted whisper of men and women now grows the fecund awesomeness of a cherry-oak tree, ready to pass through life's stages stronger and fuller – a provider for all creation. if ever there was a god, it is realized through life and love and all of this shrubbery; the marriage of life and death, of earthly heaven, of hallowed hell, of eons past – what righteousness – this universe, so chaotic in its order, even if not without its suffering.

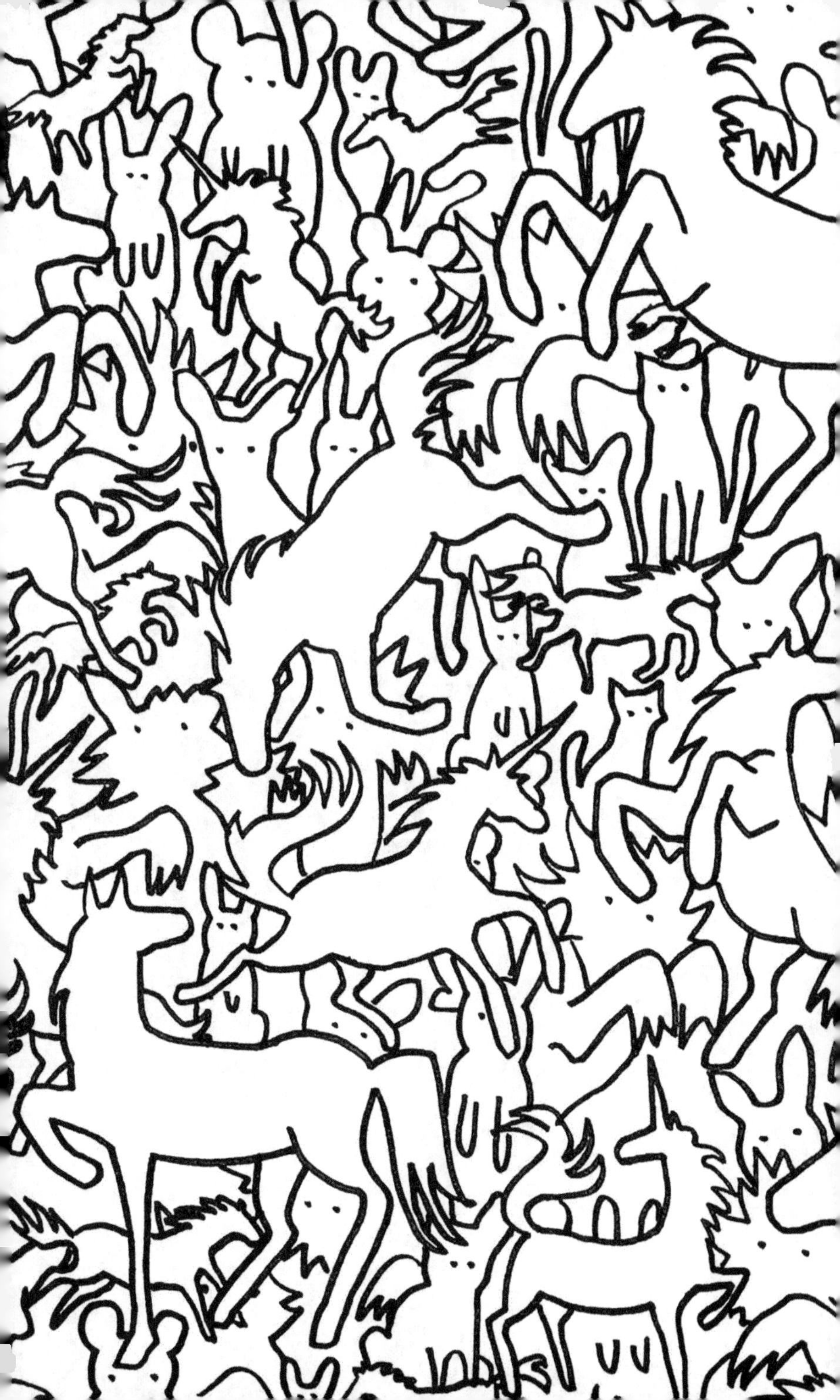

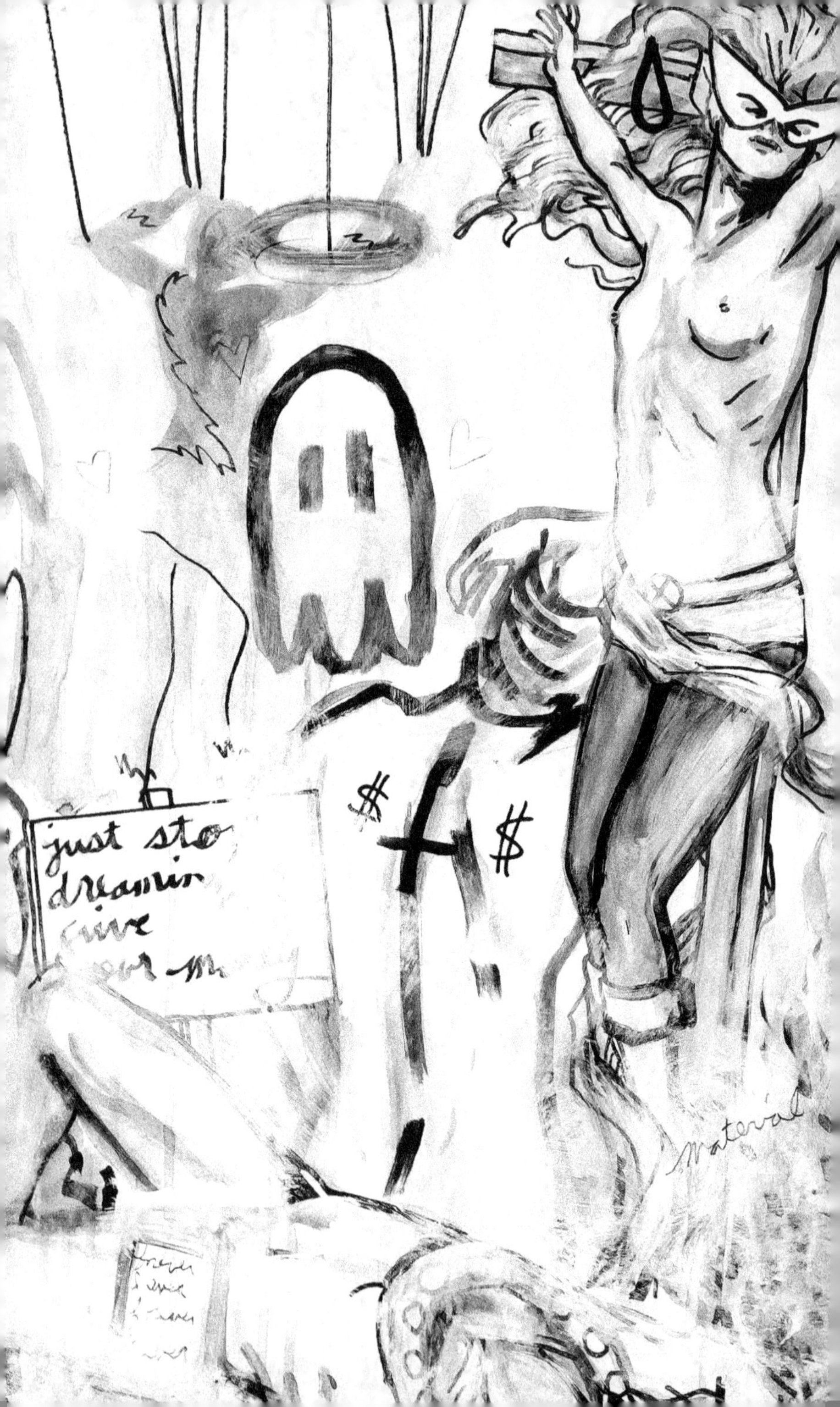
just sto
dreamin
live
our m
$
$
Material

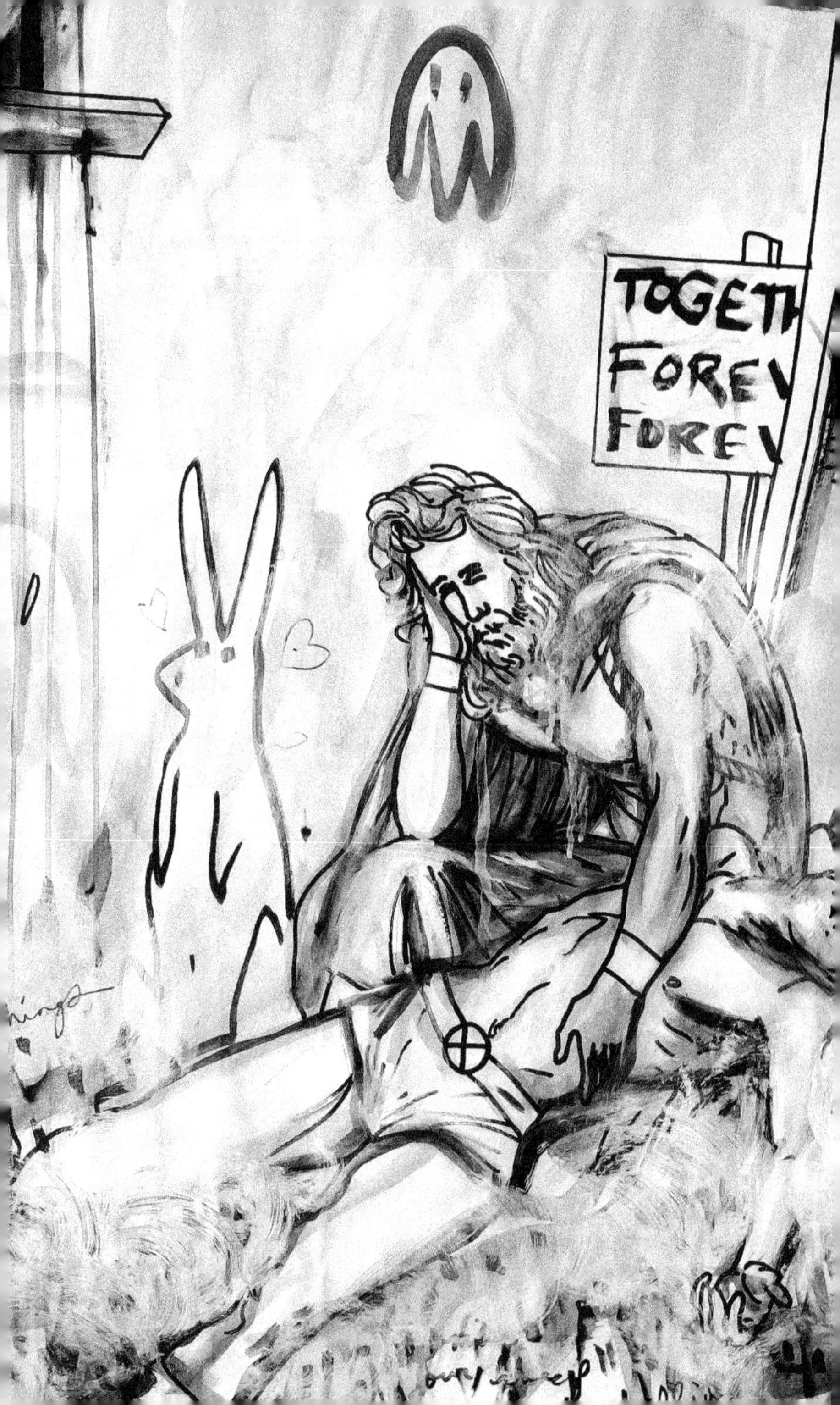

TOGETH
FOREV
FOREV

SHE SAID,
SOFTENING

now that's a heart i want to soften
unrequited but not forgotten
a dame made to blossom
back pocketed but not thought of often
i bet cocaine could get us talking
a monster, if not promising
two birds on a waterbed flopping
no regrets, she said, softening.

RAISON D'ÊTRE

to have my name painted across your lips
those little love letters of tempered bliss
searching softly and sealed with a kiss
oh, what a fool you'd be to miss
your single solitary reason of being.

so wake up from that stupid dream
put one foot into that cold winding stream
take a chance on something so pristine
oh, what do you have to lose?
your single solitary reason of being

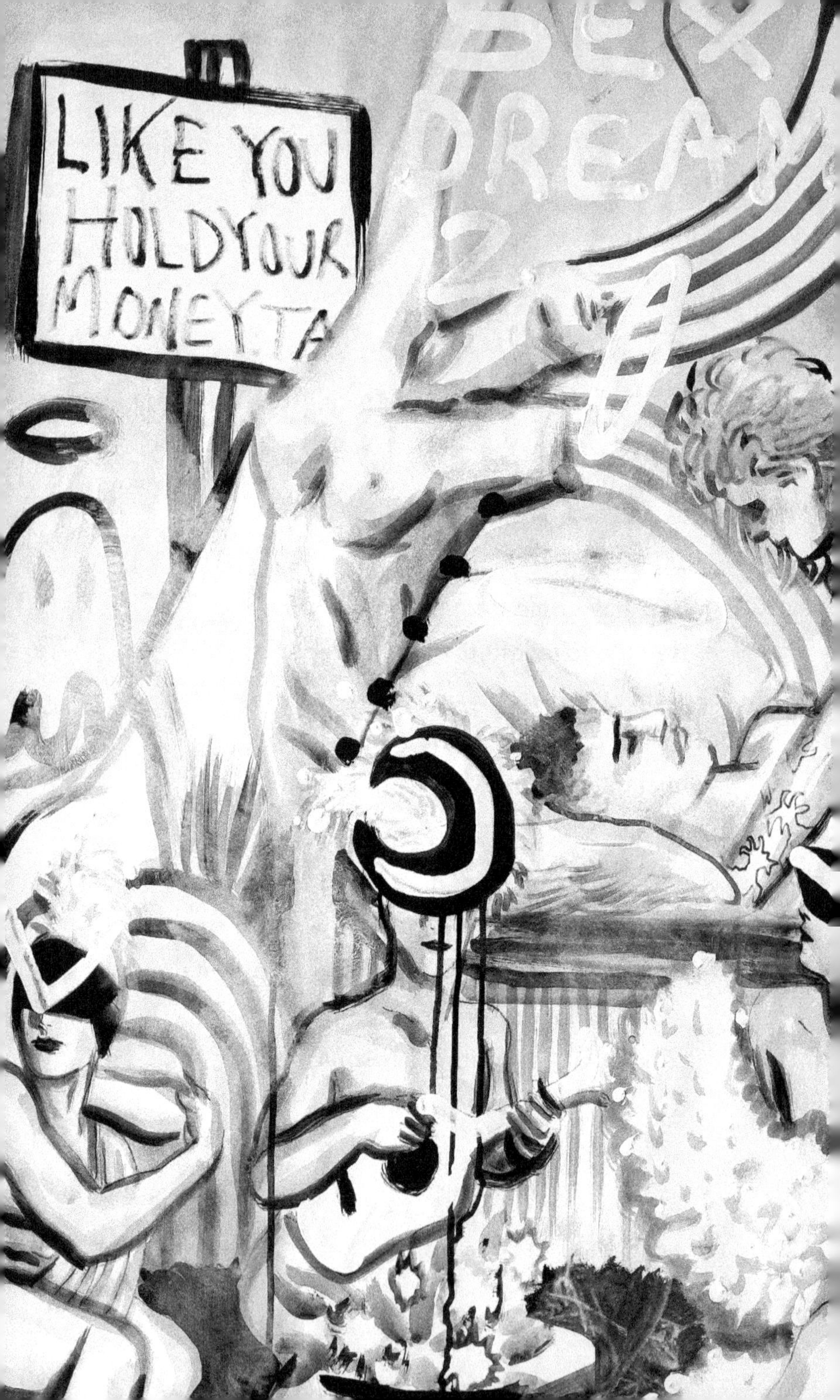

LIKE YOU
HOLD YOUR
MONEY TA

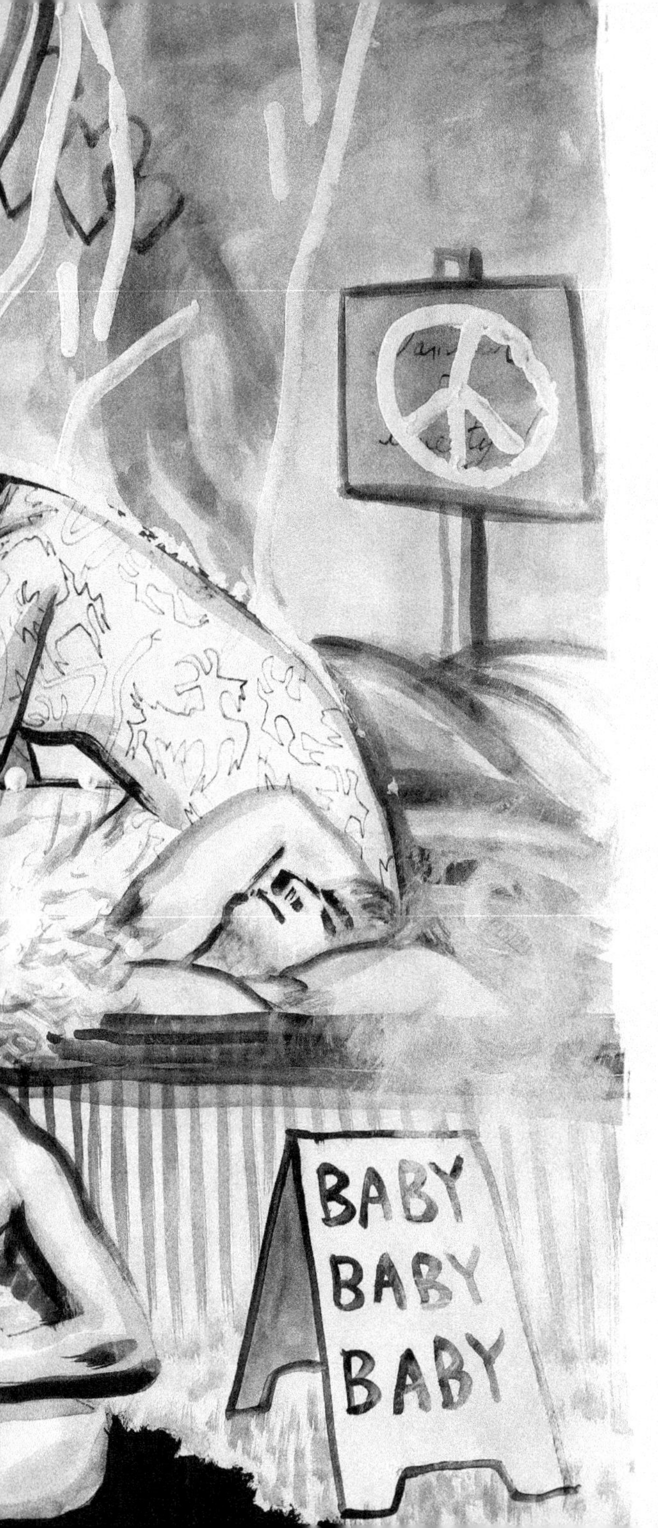

BABY
BABY
BABY

THE HUMAN CONDITION IS ABSURD BUT CHARMING

as skylarks
fly through life unbent
and people
feel their lives unspent
the absurdity
starts to boil builds beyond
the dregs of time
with a not-so-subtle hint
that this far-fetched cosmic
tale of mine
will end.
and yet
in the dust
and in its wake
there was still
something
of a shape
that left behind
a heart so full
of humans
who loved
marigolds.

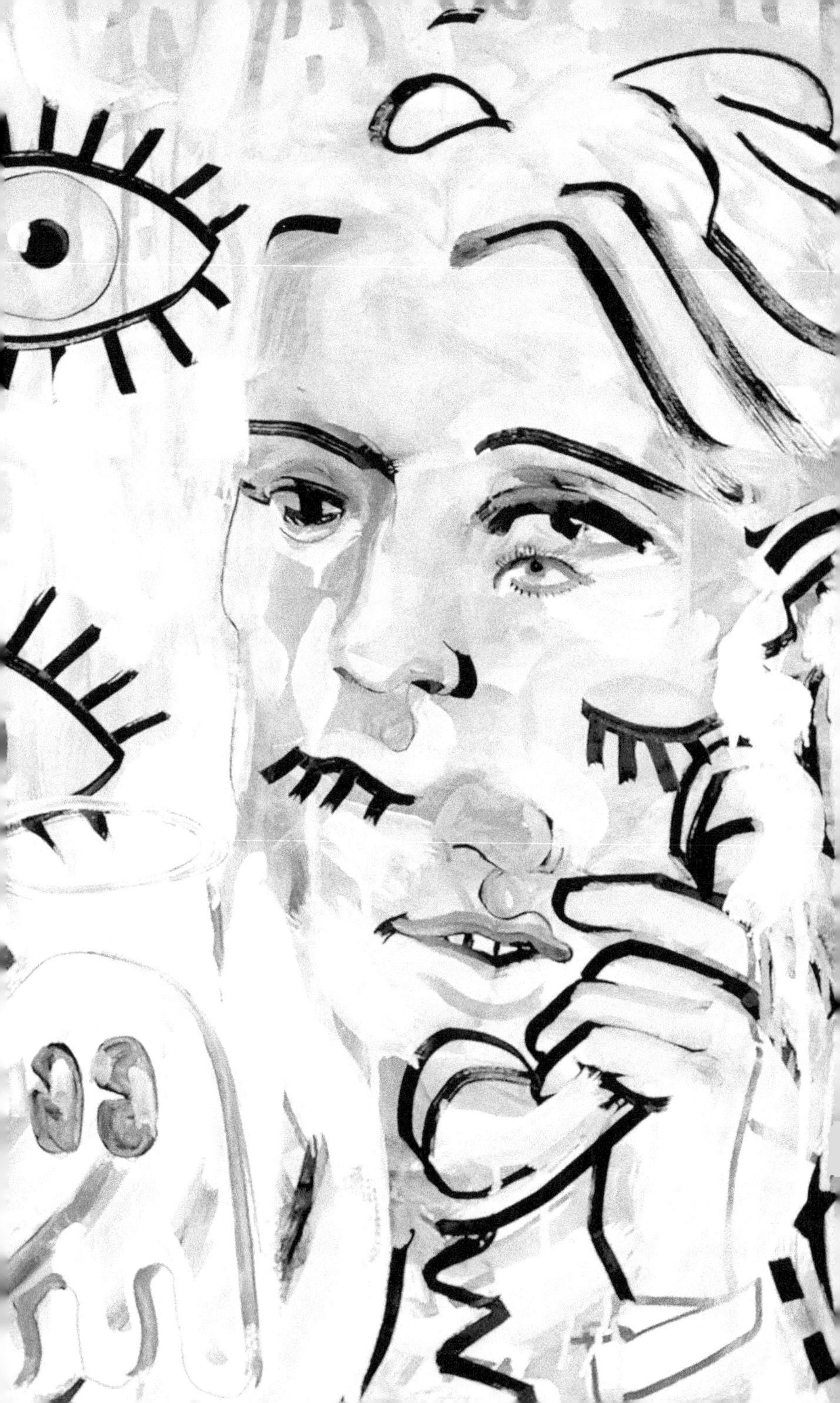

THE LAST GOODBYE

you say to me in last light
that there still lingers
something of a someone
a whimper in eternity
an empty room
where your head
once slept
once occupied
where those particles
our particles
shared the night
little giving gifts
to remember you by
because i know
you know
we all know
you're never
coming back
this is
a last goodbye.

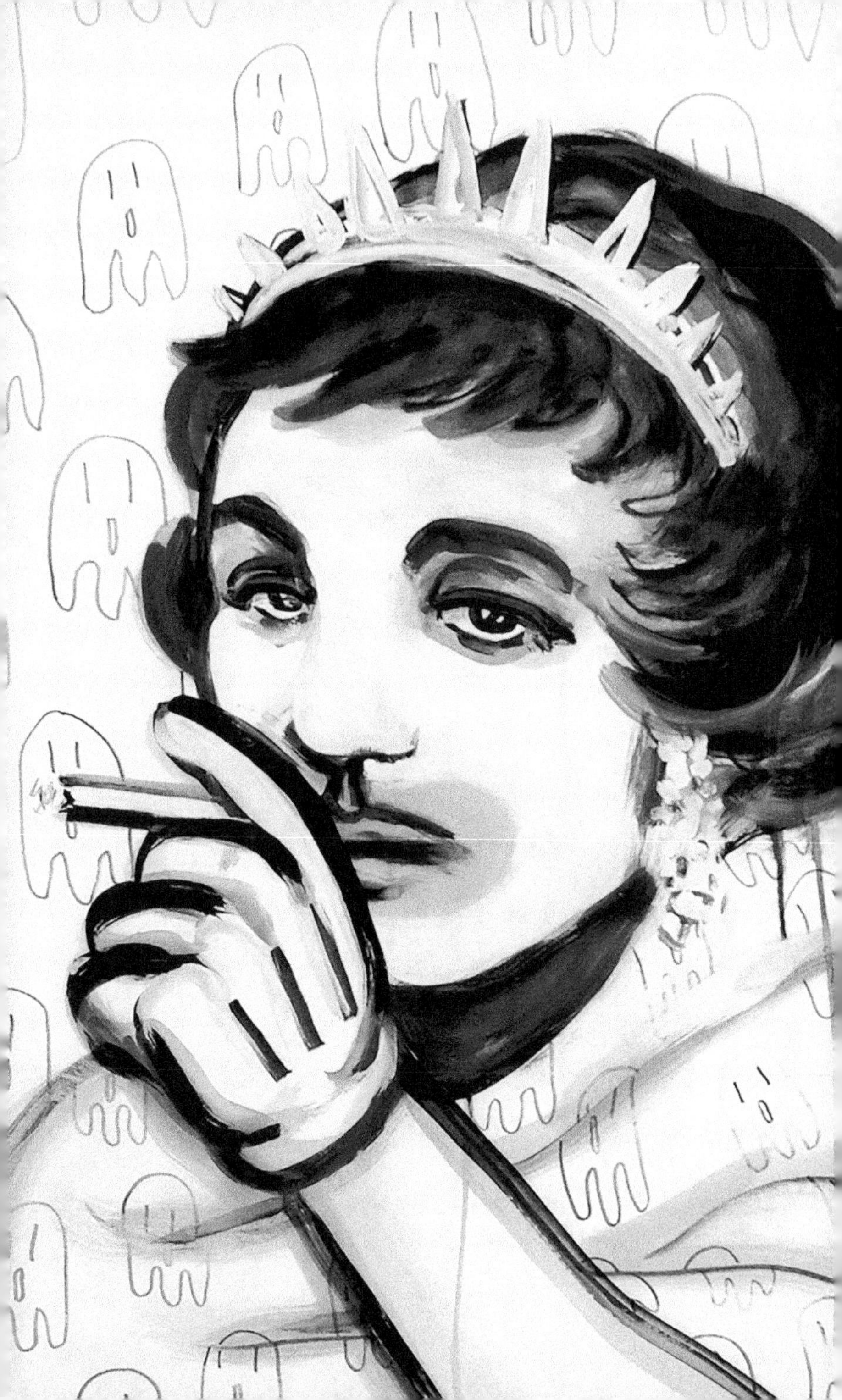

CHIMERAS

we should be
you and me
as mythical as possible
like chimeras
eternally fused
just bodies
two bodies
on body
on body
on body
this might be love
i think it's love
or it's only fucking
or orgasm
or whatever
it's nothing
where are my pants?

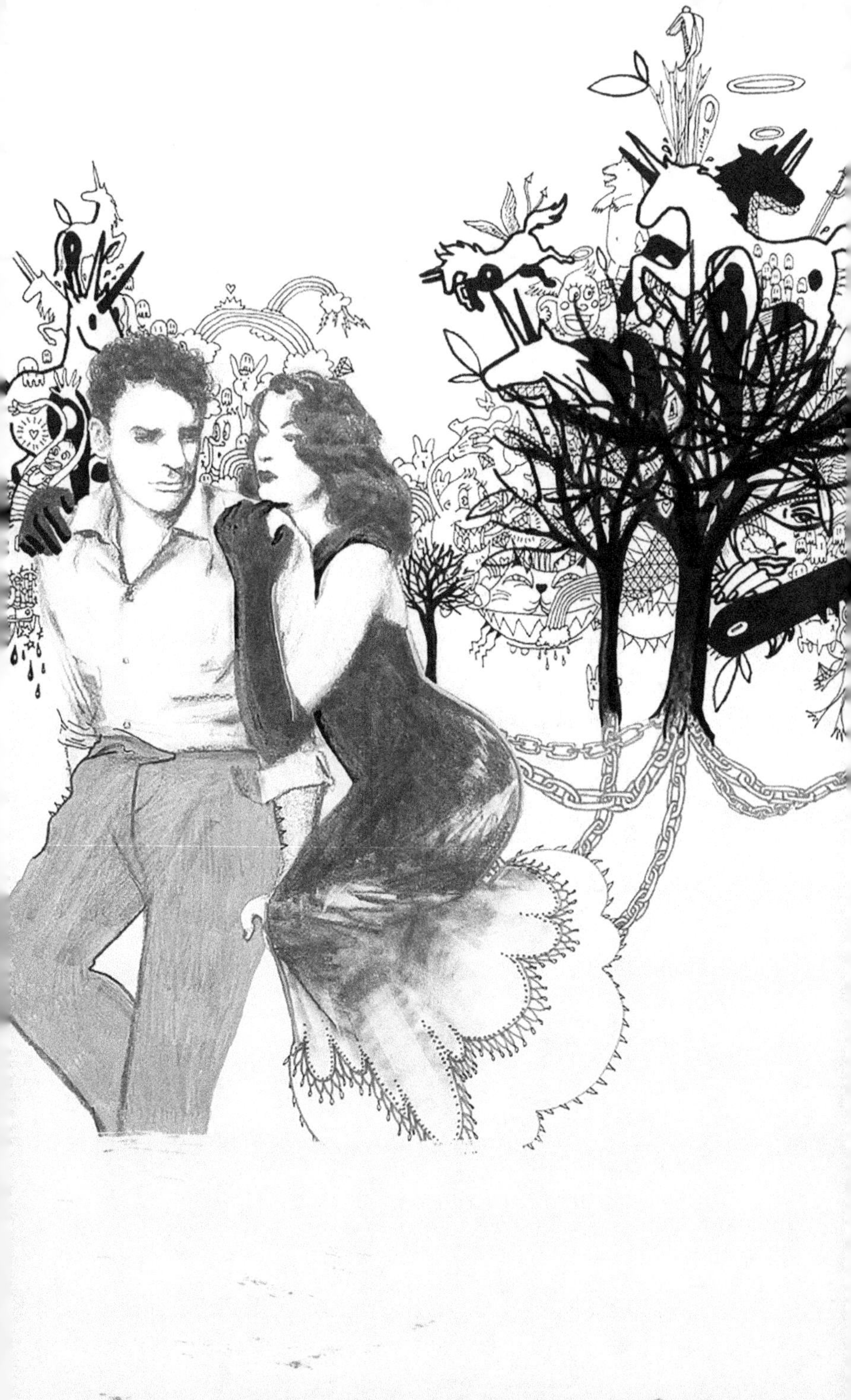

MONSTERS, TITANS, GIANTS

just remember, son
even great men
spent their fair share
of days
clinging to their
bed sheets
dry-mouthed
hung over
monsters of men,
titans of our time
giants of the mind,
they, who could bleed,
just as you and me
from the point
of a needle
a sharp-tongued word
they, who were lonely, lost, and
by god, some, most, all
every last one
afraid
of who knows what.
but --
and this is important,
my boy,
now's no time for excuses.

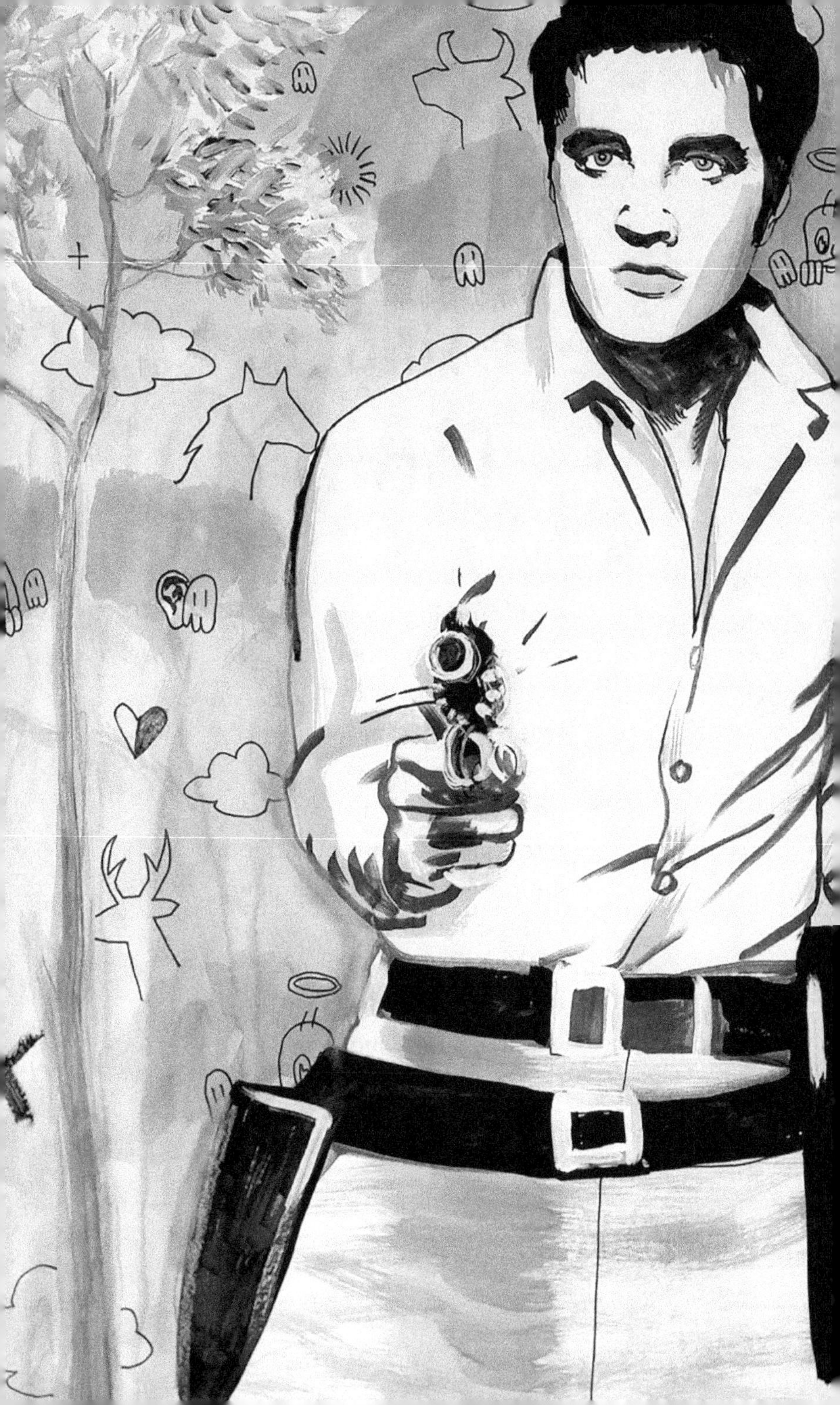

A SINGLE MAN

you lick the air of solitude
that forgiving gentle breeze
that haunting lonely prison
a place all your own
where many a mankind
have fallen into
greatness and or despair
through the sweat borne toil
the far reaches of your mind
until bones broken you
break blood from stone
while trying not to wonder
will this finally make me
feel not so fucking alone?

A LiFETiME OF IDLENESS

i'm surrounded by the minds of men

corrupted by their insatiable desire to feed and be fed,

to live their lives like creatures of the starry sunken night

to limp and claw and fight their way to salvation

what sweet angels these men are! what beasts!

crazed fluttering beasts of the worst and best kind.

and do not think yourself different or apart or freed!

you are as much the simple shackles of your inclinations.

the same horn studded demons who will stop at nothing

but the immutable laws of their own momentary desires.

who screech and pull simply for the bottom dollar of
their best friends feeding frenzy.

who bare their souls to anyone who would listen to an
inch of their speech, for an ounce of their time and not
one second less.

who plead for a purpose to a thousand gods
of a thousand false religions.

who live their lives in the tepid frustration
of untarnished hands and wasted minds.

who are neither loving friend nor foe but everywhere
in-between and who ask themselves, in quiet damnation,
will we ever change?

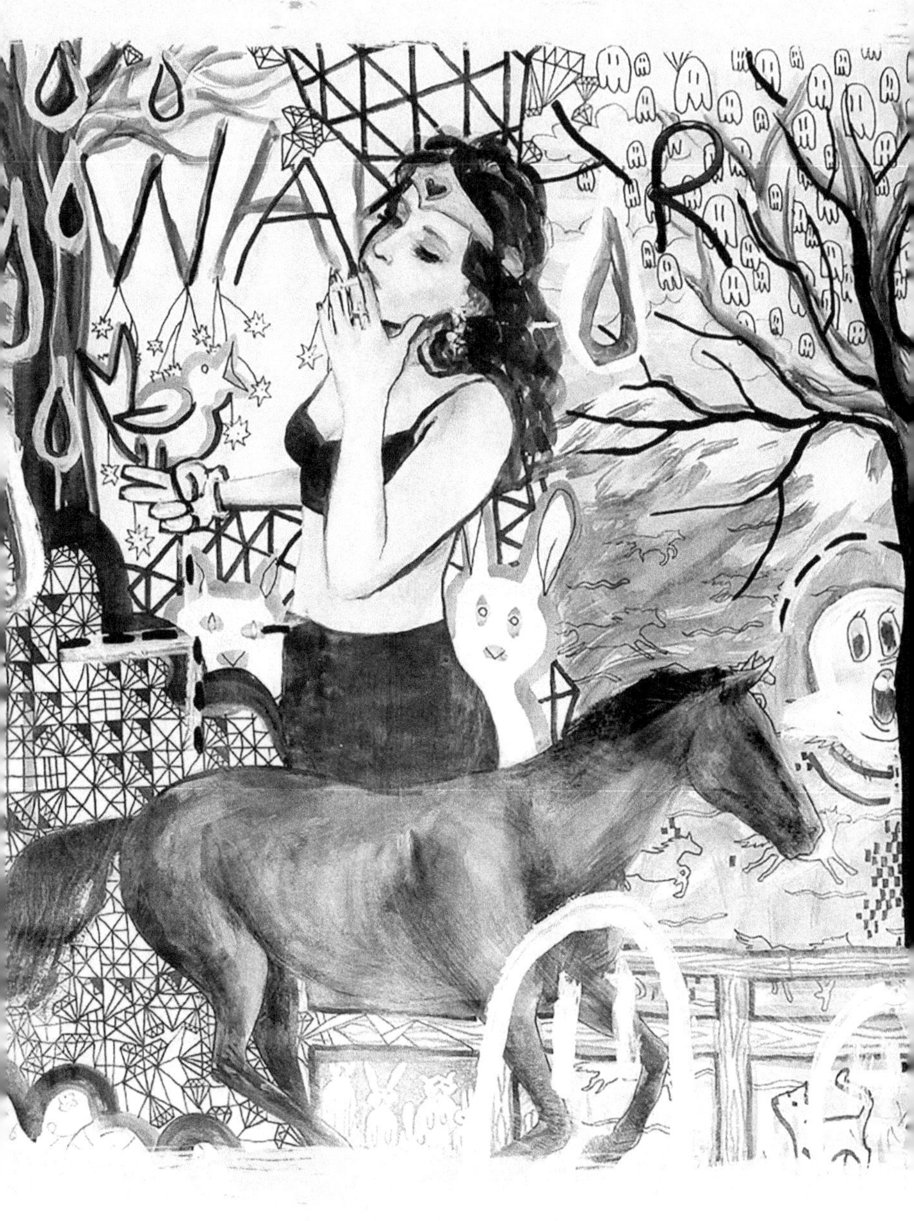
WA
R

BRICK WALLS

she said your brick walls could soften
she said we're just two people talking
she said why don't you come by more often?
she said it hurts when you don't come knocking

she said you'll be my next chapter
she said when i'm with you there's so much laughter
she said you're my happily ever after
she said sorry, i met another man i'd rather flatter

he said your words are making me weepy
he said i think you've deceived me
he said being around you two makes me queasy
he said fuck it, i ain't about to go down so easily

he said i cannot, will not believe it's hopeless
he said i know your love for me wasn't bogus
he said one day i'll make you my magnum opus
and then this poem will just be a bonus

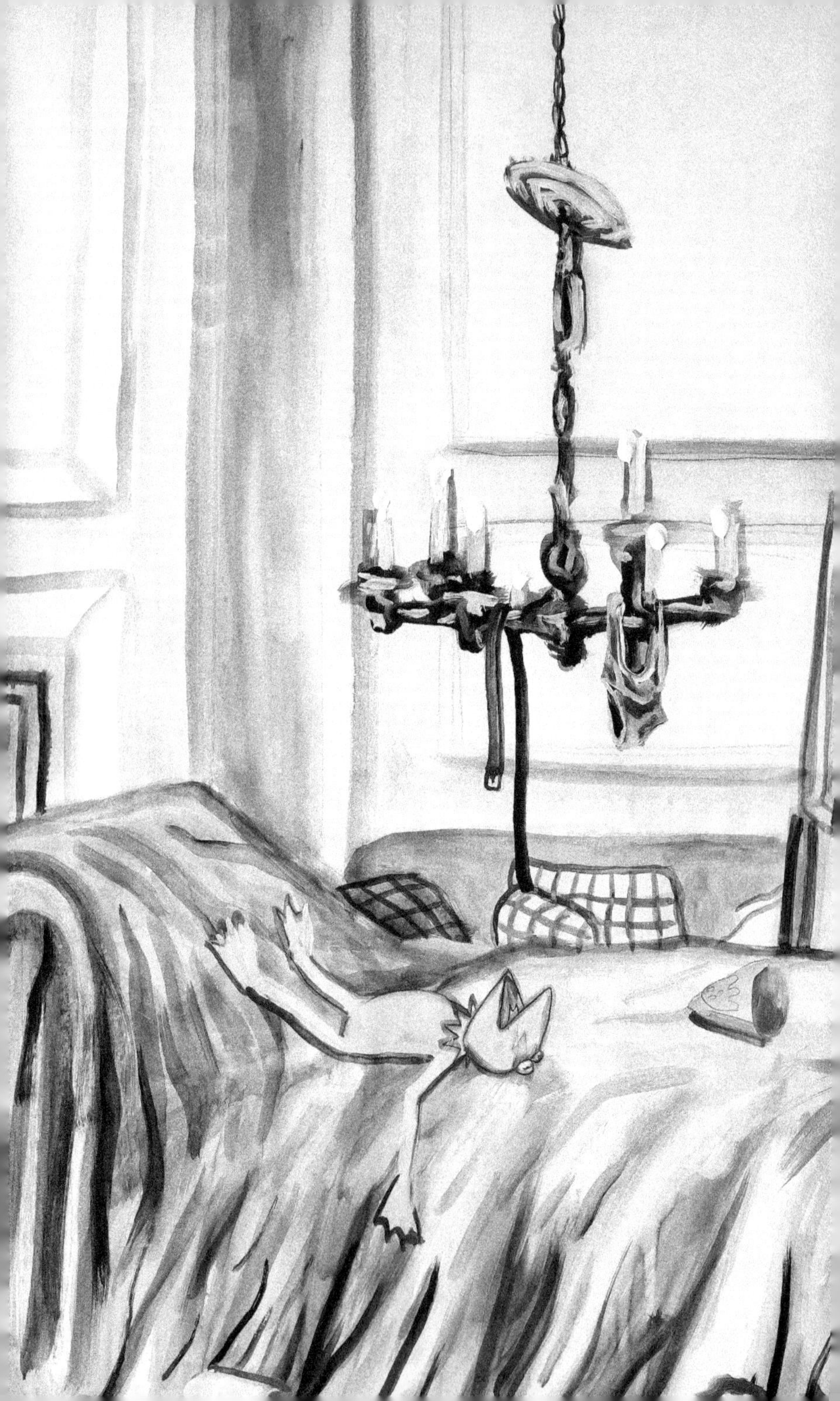

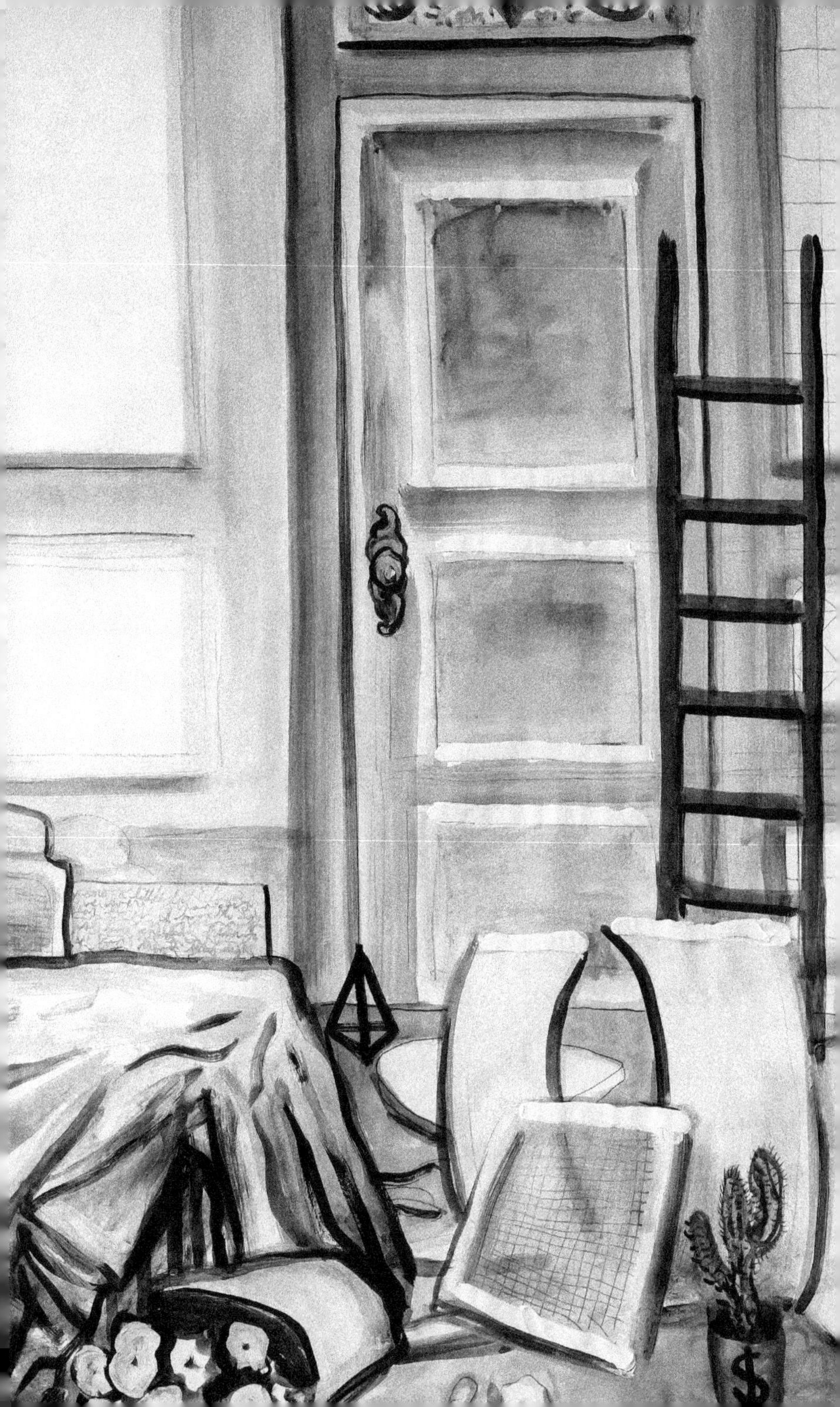

SUBLIMITY

despite the enduring inevitable ending
of this no good, rotten universe
you can't help but sit back
and gaze into the steady black flame
breathing in its putrid smoke
and feel like you were better all for it
that your life, however crooked
still managed to put a jagged tooth smile
on that god damned face of yours.

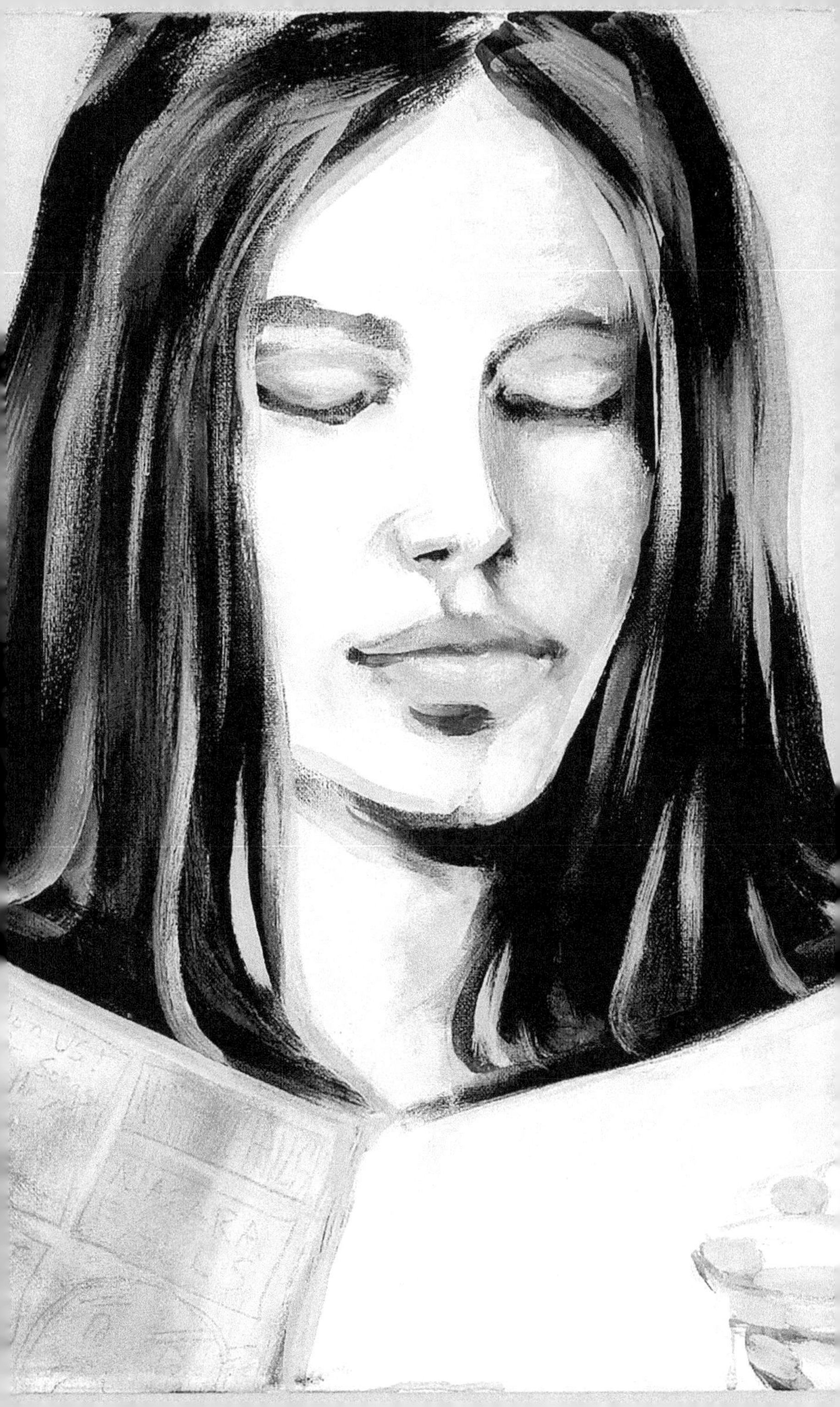

is
ART

you extend your mind
to whatever shall come
leaving that blank space
that unfilled void
open and ready to receive
through the vastness of oblivion
the god given words
of a fiending appetite
until something someone
speaks to you
the words of a madman
no! ye redeeming master!
ye borderguard of fate
of nature and existence
appearing like fragments
dust in the ostensible
careless universe
letting them
impart on you
the all knowing
power to move
to feel
to give.

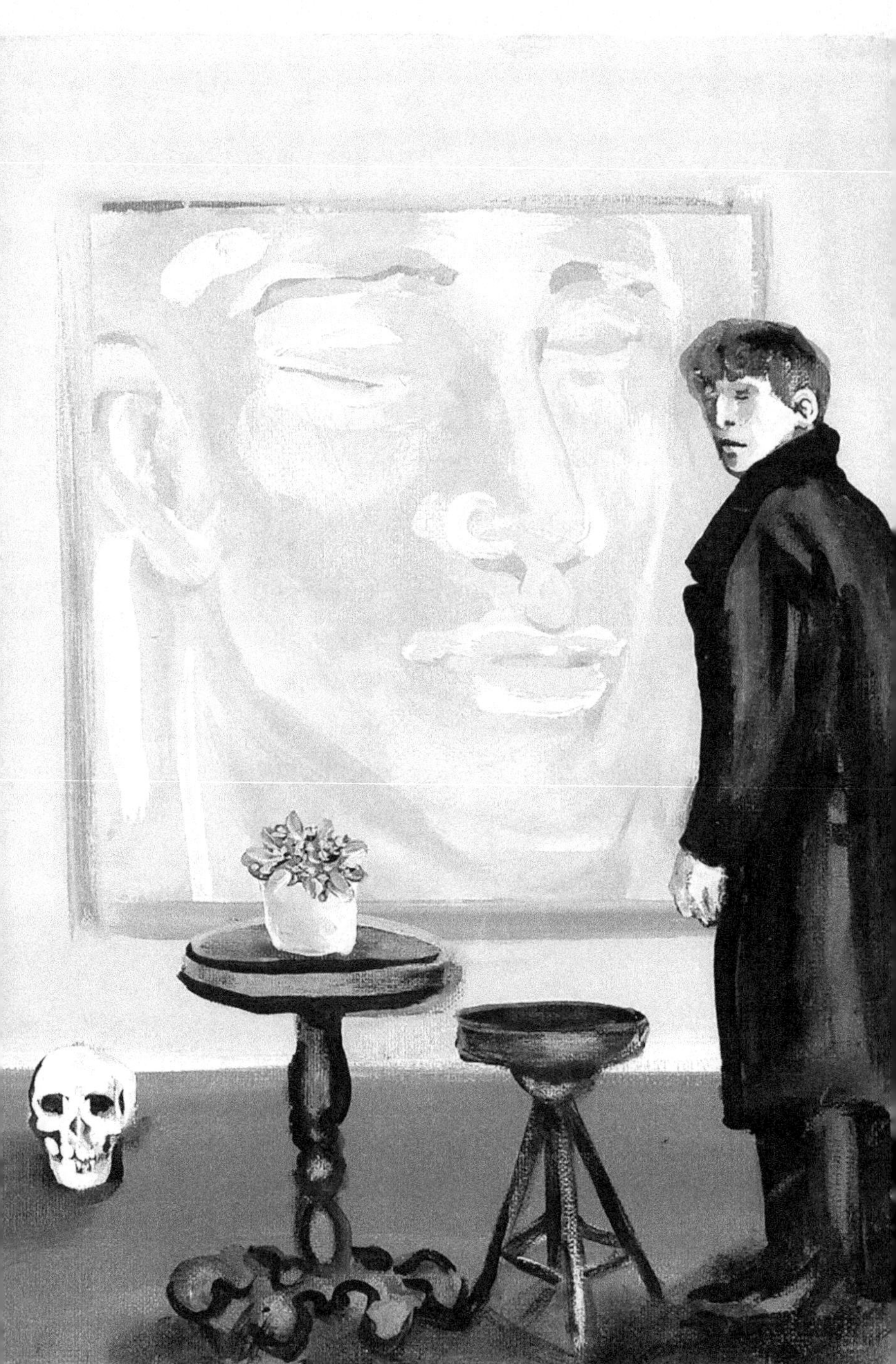

TWILIGHT

for those
who are
concerned
only with
the state
of becoming
and have
neither
a desire
nor a need
of being

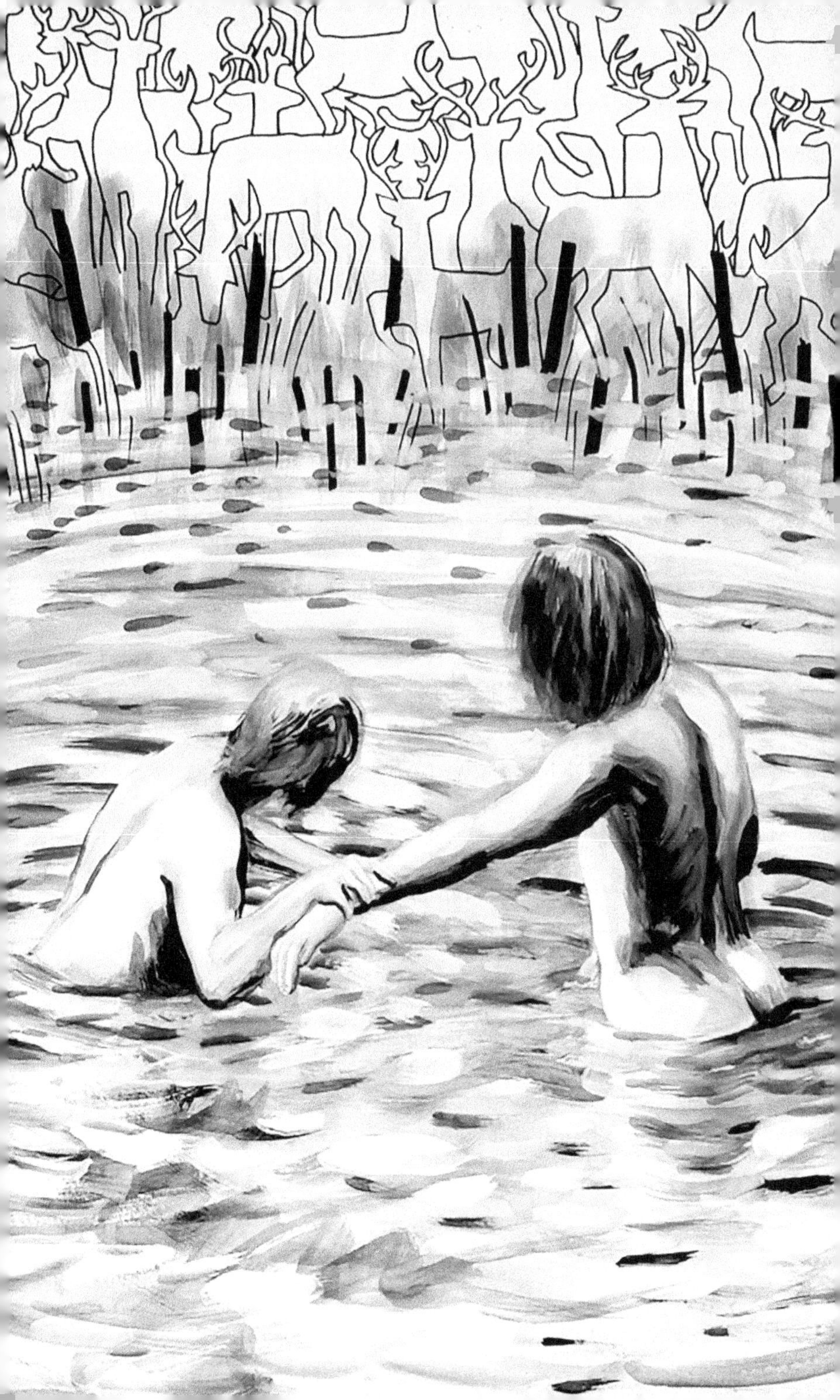

FALL APPROACHES

i will wallow
in the shrinking days
of a city whose trees
undress themselves idly
as a man, cut off at the knees
during the long cold nights
whose necks have strayed
beyond a teetotaler's measure
and the edges of the world
fade into rounded obscurity
and light, renewing light
has never seemed
so far away

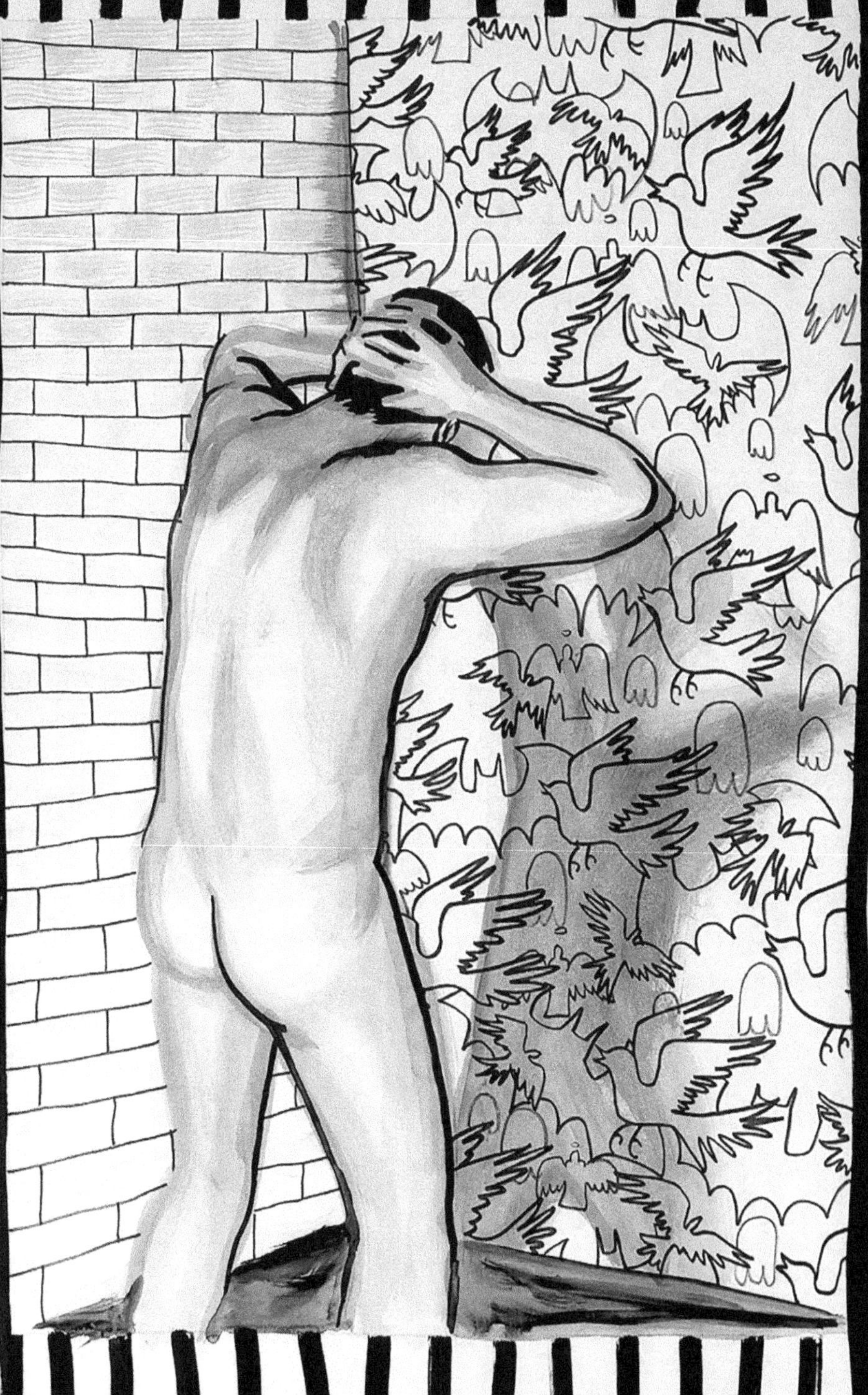

THE DAMNED HAVE SUCH BEAUTIFUL EYES

those fiery eyes!
lit up, sleepless
existing through
tonics and gin
the thin white duke.
those cracked lips!
searching for the words
"this is happiness"
and whispering,
"this is what i want."
those angels!
praising no god
no mohammedans
baring it all
and living on
the devil's whim.
this stomach!
can't stomach
all this depravity
as the burning
bright light
makes its
great escape.

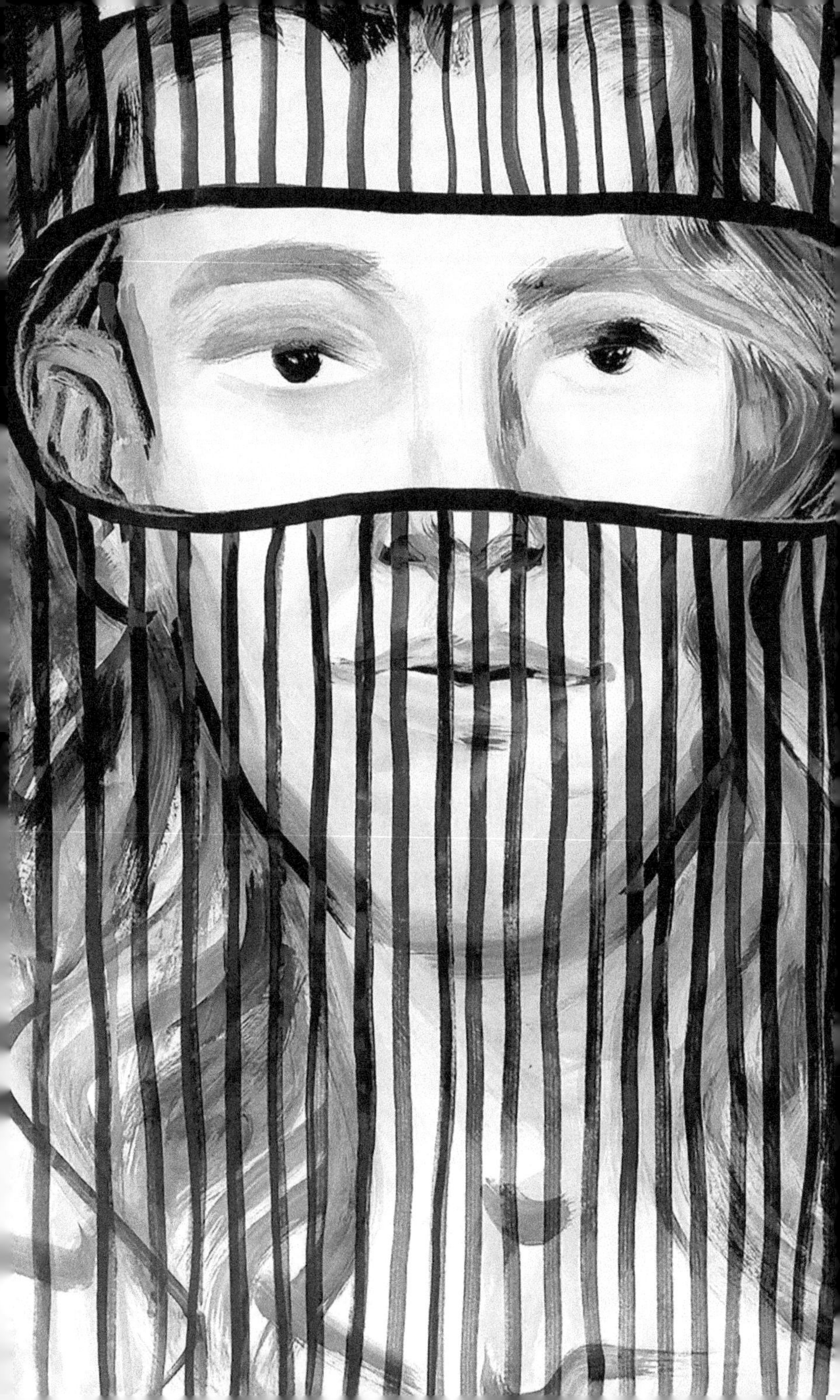

TOY SOLDIERS

tick tock and tommy guns
a ballad of a thousand sons
we're firing on —
the crying of a thousand moms
so fight your own fight
don't be such a fucking
uncle tom
serve a greater purpose
than the one you're —
gone.

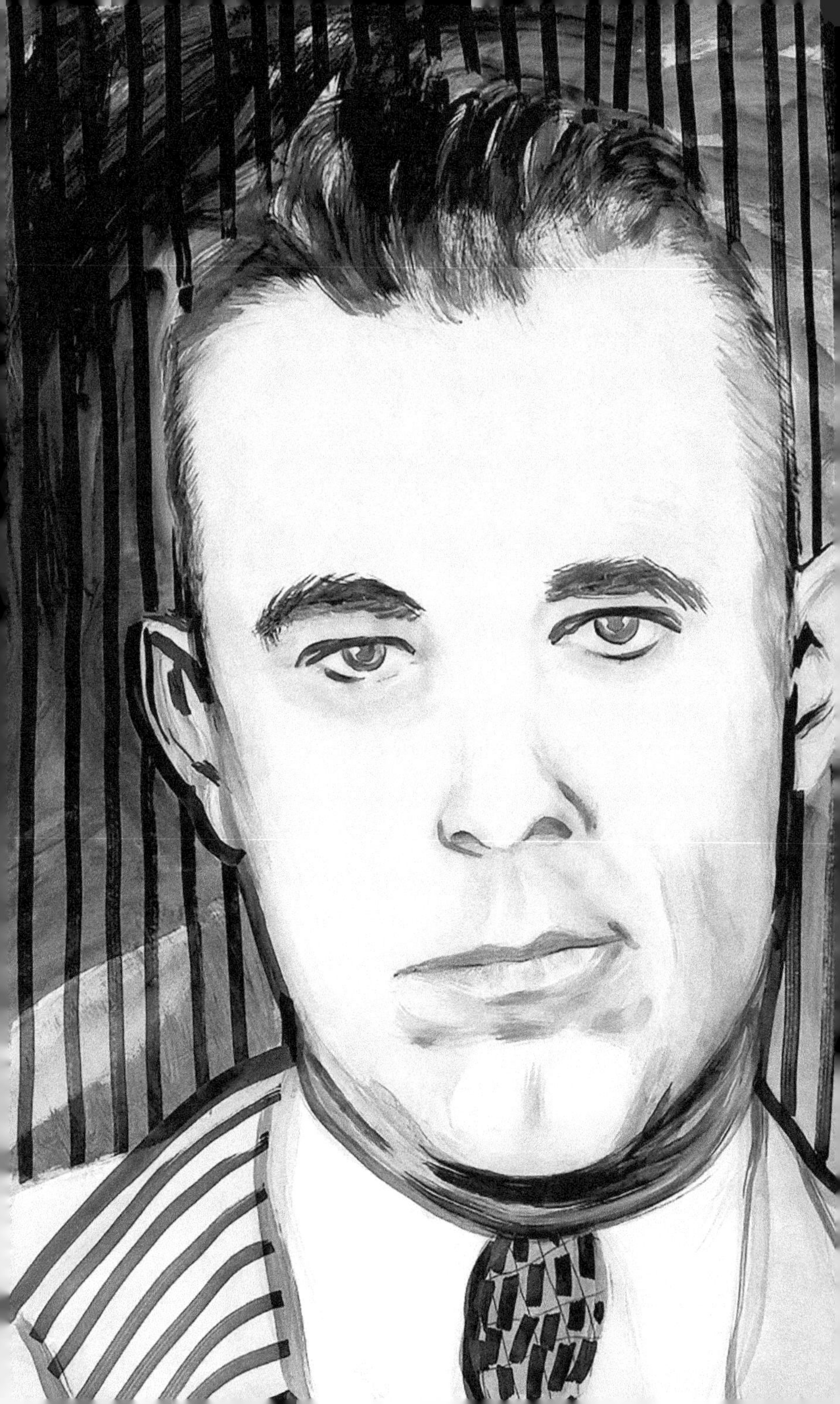

EMPTY

the winding crippling fear of the ennui
day in and day out
fixing your fix on the first hitch that comes your way
numbing yourself until you're down to your knees
abusing all your circuits just to feel a little electricity
until you're no longer a man
you're just a disease
bone stitched and broken,
you can't even sleep
so you take one last dip
just to breathe.

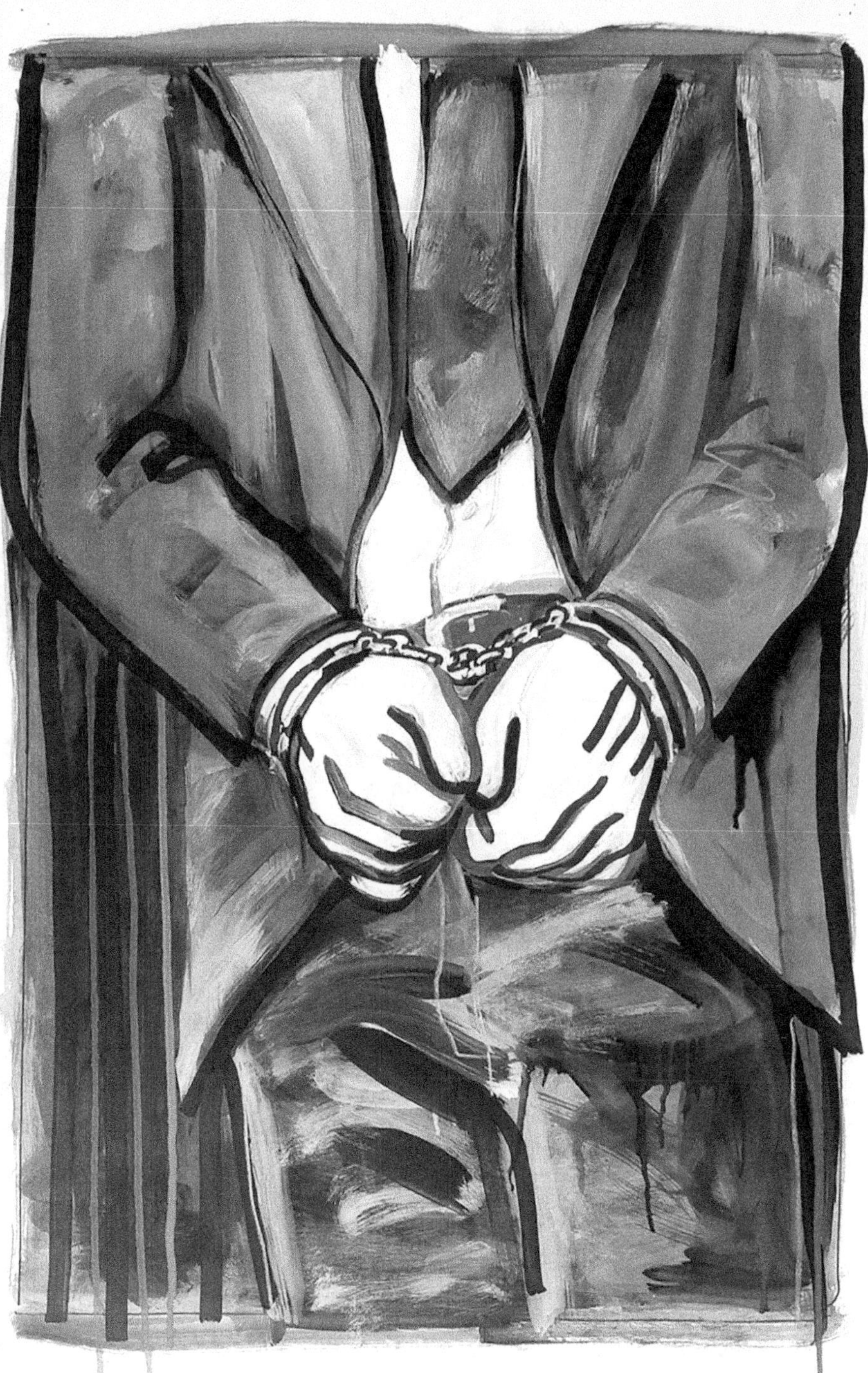

ENTROPY

what is this?

your infernal lot.

damning damnation.

listless. breathless. confused.

the void. the man.

floating through space.

just passing time.

forgetting time.

fighting time.

alone. oh so alone.

we're all so goddamn alone.

until we're not.

until we are.

an eternity alone.

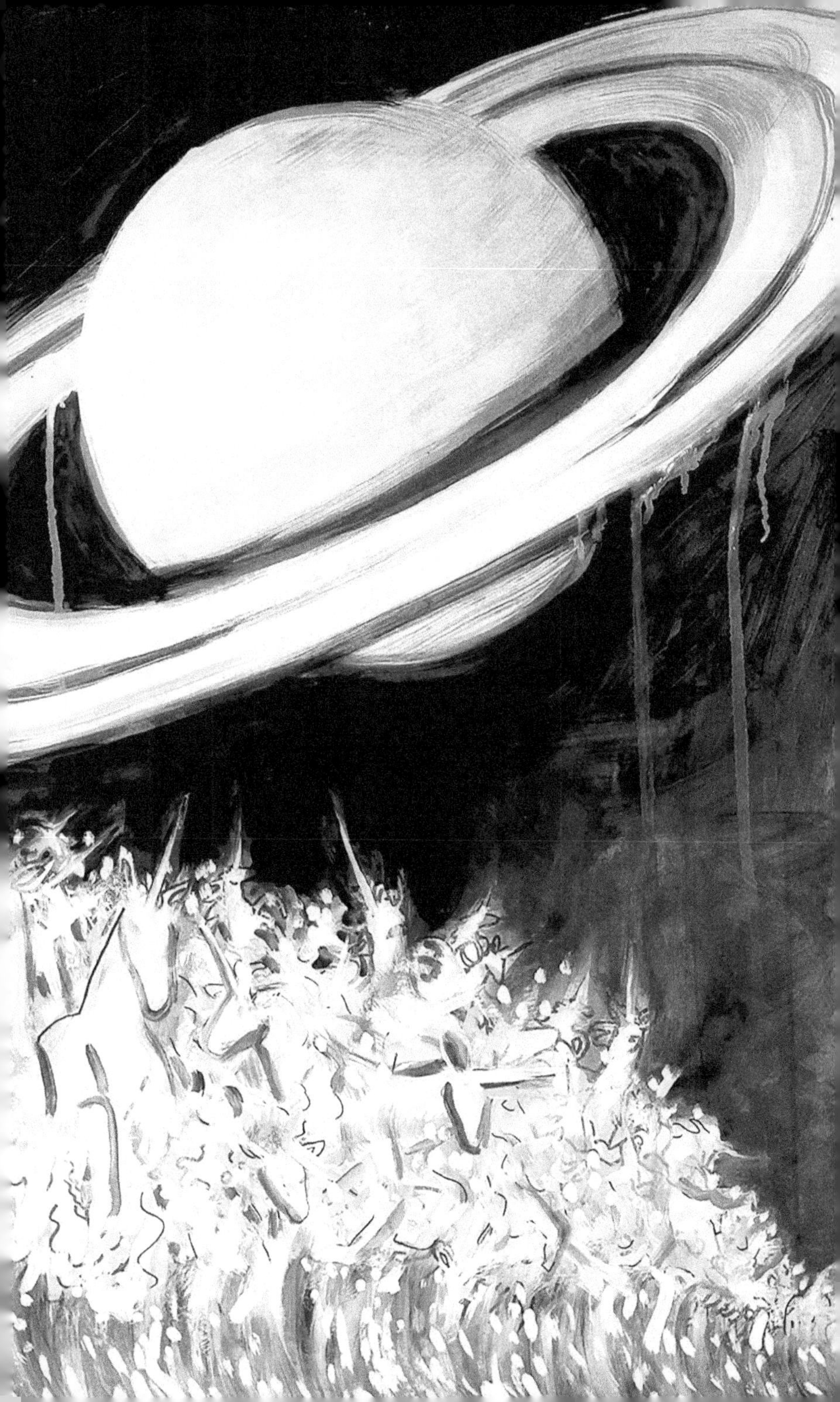

REAPER

can you outrun the reaper?
can you write a tale of his tired grip on your wrist,
asking you to come with?
telling you a fable, of the merry lands he will give?
of a life without life, of a place never lived,
of a time out of time, can you resist?
can you outrun the reaper?
i think you'll give in.
i think you'll tell stories,
only to him,
you'll run out eventually
and have nowhere to spin
because the tales you once had
have come to an end.

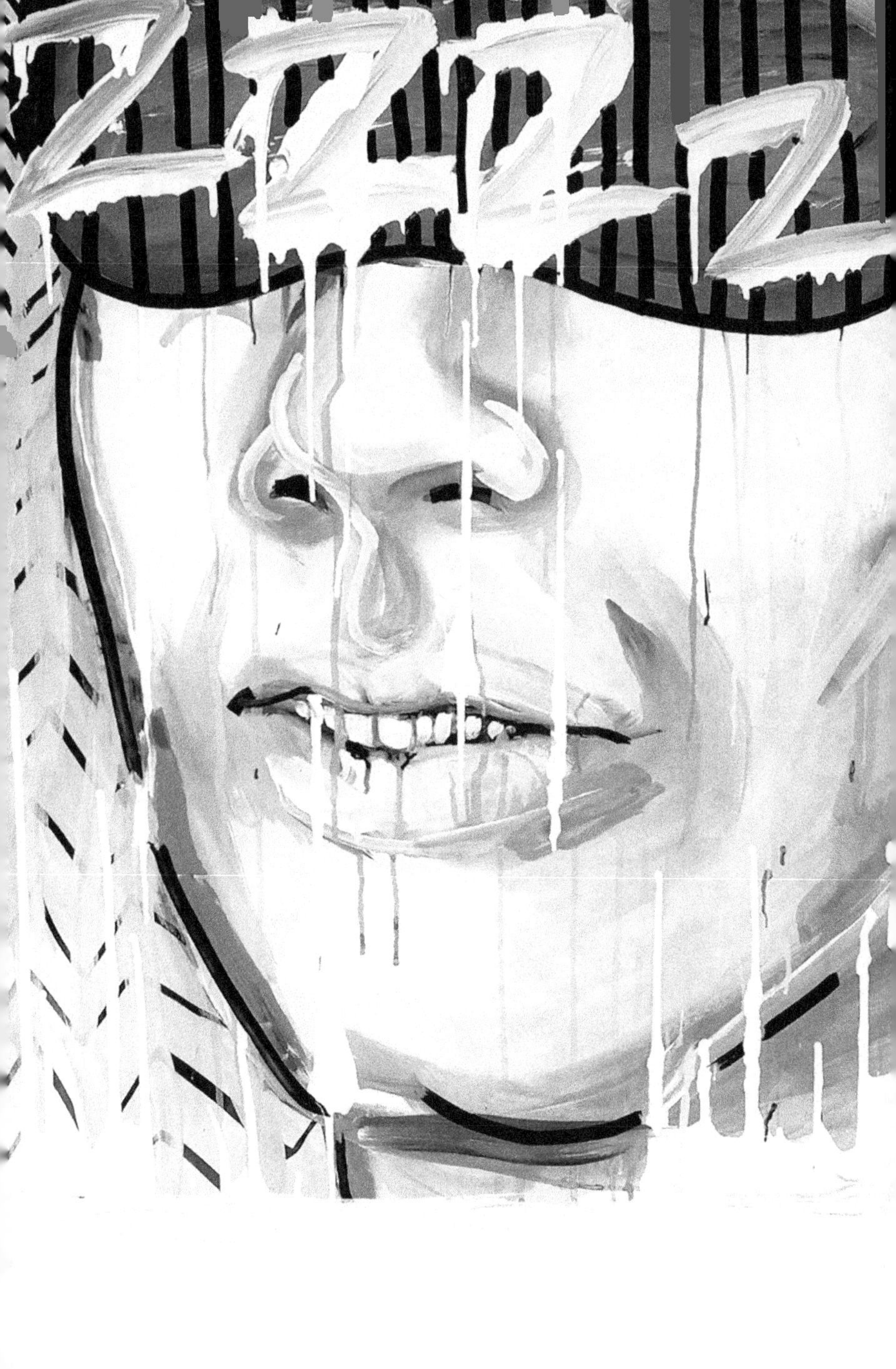

hearken back
to a place in time
where demons devils,
demigods and angels
weren't whittling men away
to red bone rust
and their souls were
yet to be for sale and sold
into the clutches of modernity

a time where the future was just
a speckle in a black endless sky
the bright guiding light
in an unknowable foggy night
an open system of possibilities
for their wandering entropy
boldly begging to be
sailed, sought and seen

and yet, now, they walk around
with one squinting eye
deaf men leading the blind
chasing the white dotted line
three by seven dollar sign
punching the card in their mind
asking is this where i'll reside?
is this where i'll die?

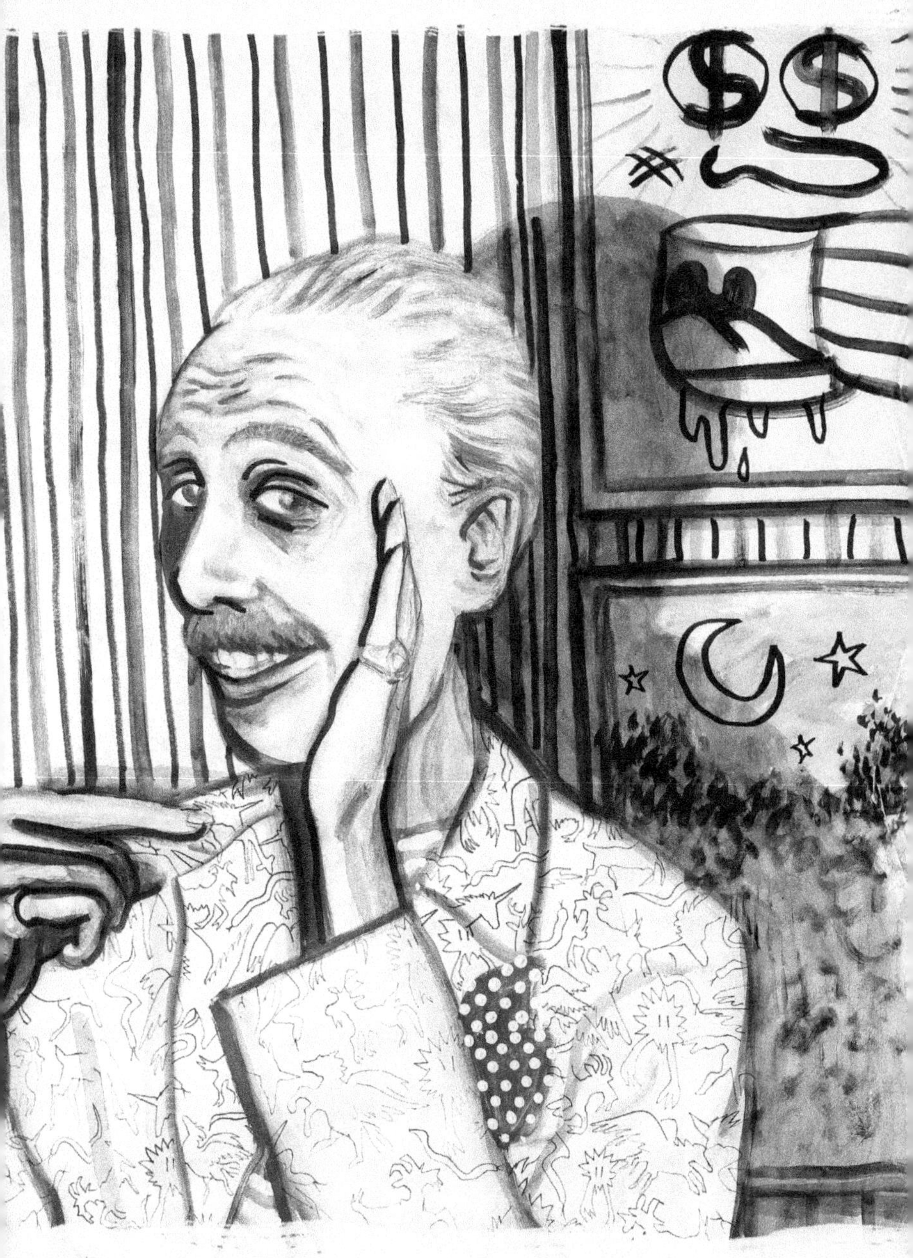

DO ALL YOUNG WRITERS

do all young writers start out as liars?

do they promise themselves their words will be fire?

do they feel greatness in veins made of wires?

only to end up so fucking tired

do all young writers search with mildewed virgin eyes?

do they bleed more than blood but pure purple passion
for a fictional prize?

do they stay up late to bask in delusion, to fantasize,
but still won't sweat for even a dime?

no they won't pillage, steal and rape for a leg up
on a generation wrapped up in their own mind

where are all the young writers who know where and
what's sublime?

where all the young writers who take greatness in stride?

where all the young writers who are burning up inside?

why do all these young writers rather fail than die?

oh how I wish they weren't I

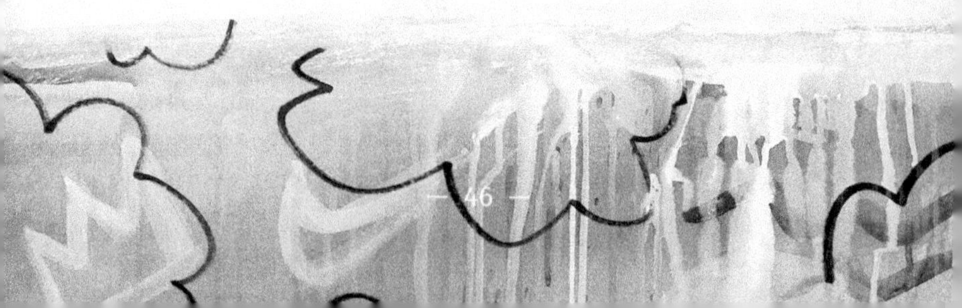

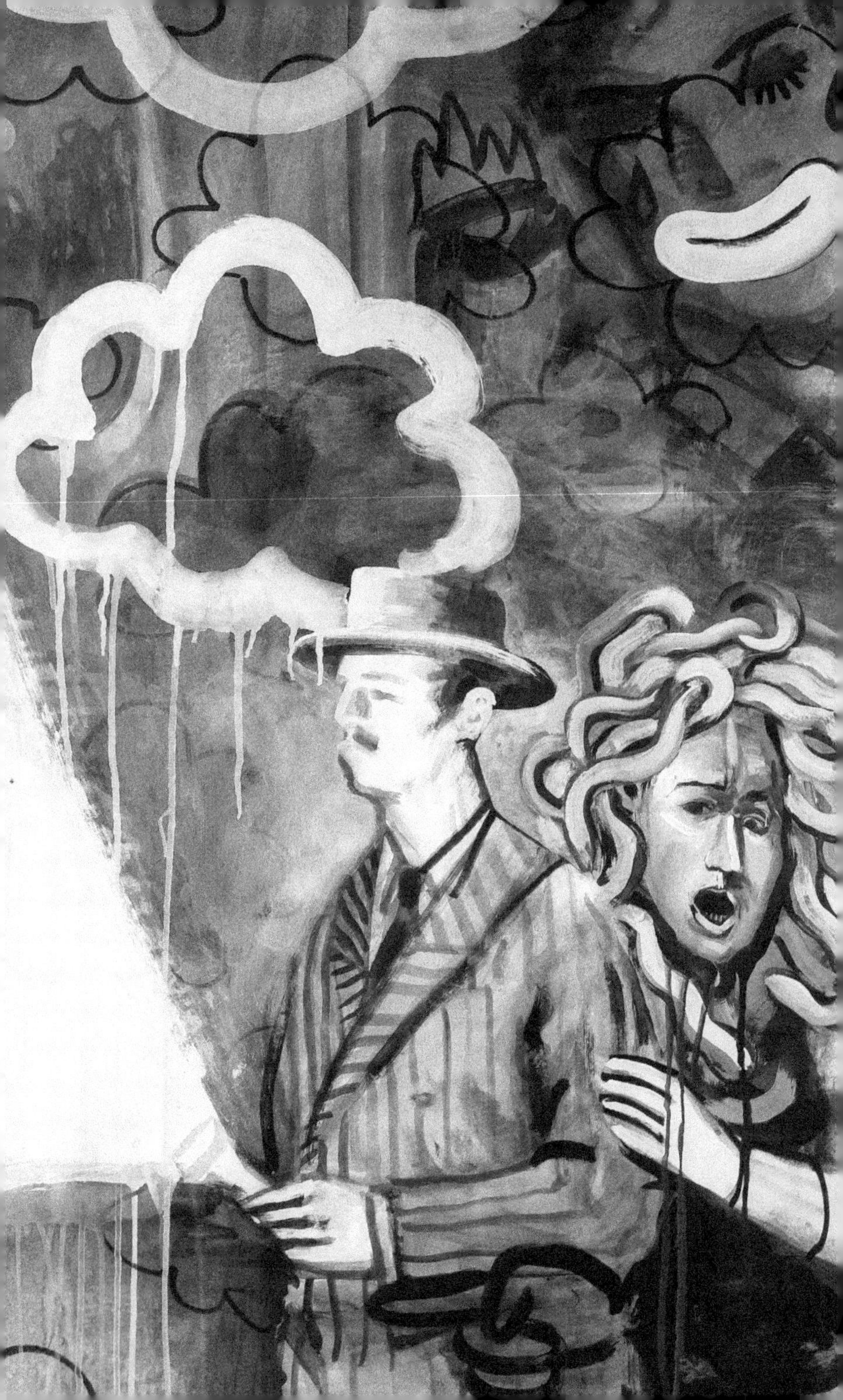

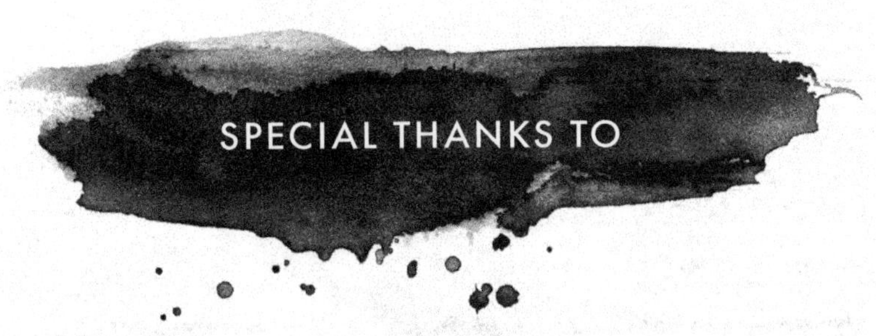

KATYA WORBETS

on holding our green hands through
the book design process.

+ PHOTOGRAPHERS

CAITLIN VARRIN
AND BRENDEN DERVIN

for turning our paintings
into digital copies.